Simply, M.E.

MICHIYA ENGLISH

Presentation by *BookLeaf Publishing*

Web: www.bookleafpub.com

E-mail: info@bookleafpub.com

ISBN: 9789357619462

First edition 2022

To you.

The only one who loved me with a love that I didn't deserve, but needed more than anything. Mimi will always love Her Noa.

Existence

What else is there, if not here in this place with
you?
Who would I be if I couldn't be yours?
You're my heart.
My sense of peace.
For as long as there's you
There will be a me

Summertime Sadness, but All Year

I just knew I'd have you

Always, always, always

Don't you know I would have given everything.
If the universe would have just shown me.
I swear this heart beats for you.

Always, always, always

And when the wind blows I can feel you
breathe.
I can't just let you be a memory.
I try my hardest not to let them see me cry.
I wait until I sleep.
I try my hardest just to smile and lie.

Please come back to me

Sofa Sleeps

I adored you most in those moments
When you were so still and at peace
When the soft whistle of the wind created the
sweetest duet with the thumping of your
heartbeat
When the tiny flickers of candle flames danced
across your face
I embraced the beauty that came with simply
having you in my space
I needed nothing more than those moments
For in those moments I could appreciate you in
the tiniest ways
And though you didn't realize it,
That's all I needed

Conversational Comfort

Place your worries at my feet
Allow your mind to be at rest
No, every problem can't be solved in one day
But you can release them into the atmosphere
and lessen the hold on your heart
You are enough
Trust these words
Take comfort in knowing that even at your
lowest you always have my care and
compassion
It's a start
Concern yourself with the good you're doing
Be not deterred by the things that have yet to be
done
In time it will all fall into place
Run to me
Do not aimlessly wander
The world is merely a series of distractions
waiting to surround you
Seek me within your spirit
Create a world for us to coexist
A harmonious balance between your will and
my grace
Take time even when it seems inopportune
I will always meet you where you are

Tilted the scales may be
But only for a moment
Clarity comes when you least expect it
Speak to me
Continuously
Regardless of how you think it sounds
Circles will eventually bring you back to what
you may have missed before
You are enough
Trust these words
And you will always be whole

Stained

Sit with me in silence
Shout to my soul without moving your mouth
Pierce my skin with the prickly pieces of
potential that lie in front of us on the floor
Let me stain your hands with care
And without a single touch, let me leave this
reminder of all the ways I would adore you
In time it will cover you like a blanket of stars
adorning the night's sky
Fragmented twinkles of my infatuation scattered
throughout the Cosmo of curiosity
Bits of my joy sprinkled in between layers of
lust and like
I would not hesitate to move each and every
sparkling moment
One by one
Until they align perfectly for only you and I
A shimmering pathway to the bliss that I can
only imagine would exist for something so
indescribable that others would search beyond
the infinite milky ways only to discover that
This was only meant for two
There, somewhere between here and nowhere,
we would be found

two twinkles of the same star, shining so
brightly beside each other that when we
combine, our glow is something that even the
sun and the moon are jealous of
And maybe I'm exaggerating
And maybe it could all be reality
Maybe it's just as simple as sitting in silence
Or just taking the time to look down at your feet
to see the prickly pieces of potential scattered on
the floor
I only want to leave this reminder of all the ways
I would adore you
And without one single touch pour out every
jewel that lies here in my heart
Leaving your hands stained

Grief Transferred

Burdens
For certain
Have you hurting
One way or another
The weight of the world on your shoulders
You try to be God's strongest soldier
But who do you run to?
It's hitting you that life can be so fickle
I know it hurts more than a little
Trying to protect your heart and your mental
But until you realize it won't be simple
I wish that I could cry for you
I wish that I could cry for you
Til your hurt is through
God's word says be still and know I am
But it's tough to close your eyes and trust his
plan
You try to rest your broken heart in a closed
hand
Seems like each day finds you crying "not
again"
It's hitting you that life can be so fickle
I know it hurts more than a little
Trying to protect your heart and your mental
But until you realize it won't be simple

I wish that I could cry for you
I wish that I could cry for you
Til your hurt is through

PSA

I can accept that I am a safe space
A retreat for your weary soul
The calm within your storms
A battery fueled by love to recharge and
recalibrate
I knowingly allow myself to be used
I give, never truly expecting anything in return
But just a reminder…I am still human

Älskling

You are a wonderful reminder of the optimistic
beauty that exists when the unfathomable thing
becomes the best thing
You are a refreshing interjection in the cascade
of my incessant thoughts
You are the inkling in the back of my mind that
never pushes completely forward and yet always
stands in plain sight
You are that nostalgic feeling in my soul despite
the fact that you are new to my world
You are the only answer to a question that was
never asked
And somehow you manage to be correct within
any context even when you can't logically be an
option
 Contrary to what the brain conceives you are
always what the heart wants
And for reasons that cannot be explained I find
myself drawn to you
You challenge my notions of girlish desires and
whimsy, leaving me with the lingering feeling
that before you I only dabbled in a world of
pseudo attractions

Your presence is proof that my vision of a
paragon can be translated into reality
And effortlessly so
And you are not without your flaws, but they
seem to only solidify the fact that beauty lies in
the process of the journey to be made whole
And just as I imagine God delighted in your
creation, I find myself enthralled by the pleasure
I experience in sharing this life alongside you; in
watching you reach your apotheosis
You are the poem I could never write because
the words needed could never be found, but
rather felt
And I don't mind
For I would gladly submit myself to an eternity
of the euphoria that I drown in when I'm with
you
Simply put, you are, and that will forever be all I
need

Chain Reaction

All those feelings.
All at once.
All for nothing.
All she wanted.
All within him.
All out of reach.
All in a dream.
All in her head.
All in his touch.
All in his kiss.
All behind closed doors.
All her happiness.
All in his words.
All of her pain.
All for those feelings.
All at once.
All for nothing.

Fear of Reality

I'm afraid to verbally illustrate the feelings that
you orchestrate within the parts of me that
cannot bear to be set free to be manipulated by
sweet nothings and unintentionally wasted time.
I'm not afraid to fall.
I've done that a time or two and it proved to
provide quite a thrill.
But I'm a bit older now and find that I want
more than cheap thrills.
I don't know if you're the one, but I don't want
to risk you being just another name in my
memories.
I want to create moments with you that make us
both better people.
I want silly stories to share when we're older
with strangers who look upon us with
admiration and a hope that they could one day
mirror love the same way that we do.
And yet...
I'm afraid that you might actually anticipate and
reciprocate my feelings.
Awaiting my dive, arms open wide, heart
following suit.
What if you catch me?

Bevy of Evil & Desires

In the stillness we found ourselves covered by
sheets of wonder, amidst blankets of questions
that neither of us wished to remove
The frigid answers that awaited easily deterred
us from leaving our fortress of solitude
Delighting in the softness of our pillows of
comfort and complacency, we glanced into each
other's windows
Sun's beginning to rise, we rolled over, backs to
one another
We can never seem to face the light that comes
with the start of a new day
We lie here side by side equally unafraid to
submit to the desires of the flesh, yet hesitant to
embrace the truths within our hearts
The only magic that happens here is how
quickly we manage to allow our feelings to
disappear
The whispers of our hearts were muffled deep
within the tussled sheets of deception
We always found that too suddenly came the
twilight, leaving us in the dark again
Here in our BED

Closet Confessions

Tipsy tongues depositing sweet sober sentiments
delicately into the ears of the innocent
Pent up promises of a percolating passion now
seeping through the heart and emitting a faint
glow
Fear forced to wait in line for just a minute so
that the New Year would allow for a new way to
ignite an old flame
Time nonexistent for the moment, as if stopped
to ensure that this chance didn't pass us by
Closet confessions
And when it was over you stood in front of me
The sweetest eyes
Stripping me down without my permission
Silently exposing me to the me that I fought to
hide from you
Neither of us quite knowing what to feel, but
both of us knowing that we felt something
The same something that had lingered on our
minds from time to time
Glimpses of a beautiful future playing vividly
through your eyes
We were connected
Feeding off of the undeniable chemistry that
would forever flow between us

Two stars of the same constellation cosmically
bound and yet intertwined in more ways than
that
That magnetic pull into a clasp of comfort
always finding us
Always calling us
Always making this feel like the obvious answer
to a question that even our friends wished would
be asked aloud
And for a split second we were finally in that
place we never asked for, but knew we wanted
You were my…
And I was your…
But we weren't a thing
Something held us at arm's length
Whispered to our wishes that they couldn't come
true
And we knew they were right
We knew our chapter was still being written
Somehow we thought we'd be able to choose
our own path
But the ending has already been decided
So for now we remain nothing more and nothing
less than what we were before
An effortless connection paralleling pockets of
promise
Trusting that if it's God's will, we'll finally
intersect at your genuine heart and my
unwavering optimism

Safe Keeping

When you cross my mind
I speak to the wind
All the words my heart holds for you
I put them onto paper
I throw them away
And I allow myself to breathe a broken sigh of
relief
Knowing that I'll think of you again

Back From Bali

Absence makes the heart grow fonder
But while we were apart you up and took your
heart back to a familiar place
I could never compete with history, but you
made me fall hard anyway
And now that clouds are rolling in you want to
retreat
Control, ALT, Delete

...But will it ever be the way you think
Nothing really changed, time just went by
But a heart never forgets truths seen by naked
eyes
And yet here you go again, eyes covered, guilt
pulling you back in

What can be said when you don't truly want
what you deserve?
If we rewind and take the time I think you'd
realize
This wasn't all for nothing
Our moments were leading to something

Almost Never Counts

I felt us there...
That place where your strange and my weird
collide into an amalgamation of wonderful that
soars beyond comprehension
Neither of use dared to mention, but it was
obvious by the uninterrupted exchanges and the
lingering gazes that this newly formed creation
was destined to be something
If only we had taken the time to appreciate if for
all it could have been
Maybe we could have rewritten the laws of like
and love
Maybe we could have deceived our destinies and
stolen moment for ourselves
I felt us there...
 And there is where I wished we'd stayed

An Introduction

Welcome to the world of a single hopeless romantic. Where glances speak volumes and kisses imprint long lasting memories that can't be washed away. Where butterflies in my stomach are both desired and dreaded. Where I love you is easily transposed with "How was your day" and "What do you want to eat". Where I love you is often verbally avoided and rarely returned. In this world, the illusion being maintained is the only thing that matters to us. The comfort we occasionally create shines through the sheets that our bodies find themselves tangled in each morning. It keeps us warm on those chilly nights when all we seem to need is a non verbal agreement to get lost in one another. Perfectly Lonely and yet much happier when we're Alone Together.

Study Abroad

Remnants of you sprinkled on my skin
Reminders of the night before
Hidden to the naked eye, but forever embedded
in my mind
Journey back again
Get lost in my sea of curves
Bask in the glow of my melanin
Discover my peaks and seek peace in my
valleys
Feel the warmth from my inner core
Don't worry if you've forgotten the way
Simply start and it will all come rushing back to
you
Let my body be your map
Outline the route with your fingertips
Circle your points of interest in kisses
Take your time
And indulge in the pleasures that each
destination has to offer

G.G.G.G.G.

Silly of me.
Poor little me.
Lost in the thought of handsome old you.
Glued to your charisma and locked into your
smile.
I clearly have the time to waste feeding my soul
your broken promises and sweet lies.
Empty calories I suppose.
But all the while my heart is full of you.
And you're just full of shit.
You never said that this was a new beginning.
That this time wouldn't be like the last.
No.
My mind revised your words.
Decided to take creative liberties.
Remixed an array of your greatest hits until it
played back like a love song.
Truth be told you only stepped back in for a
moment.
Saw a chance to simply let me know that I was
on your mind.
But mine grabbed your presence and threw it to
my heart.
Forced it into her hands and convinced her that
it was ours to keep.

To build on.
To dream with.
And I know it's wrong.

Ugh

Pardon my view of this thing we're creating
My vision may be a bit blurry
I've lived my life floating in the clouds
Rose colored lenses affixed to my peripheral so
that even when glancing back I can only seem to
see the beauty within the beast known as
infatuation
I imagined myself a realist
And don't we all
But here I am
Somewhere between total bliss and an utter
disaster
Skipping to the melody created by the
syncopation of our heart beats
Breathing in an air of optimism until my lungs
are full
How quickly I might choke
But instead I exhale into a blissful calm
Releasing the particles of perfect happiness
leftover in my spirit from moments spent with
you
How easily it seems to have come to us
This euphoria that has built itself into a
promising illusion
Or maybe it's real

Your touch reminds me that it isn't completely a
dream
Your kisses imprint silent confirmation that
maybe this is just what it seems
You could be mine
You could dwell comfortably within my mind
and set up shop inside my heart and find a place
within my soul that no one has sought out before

Wishful Thinking

I long for the days when I think of you and feel
absolutely nothing.
I pray for them in fact
I lay in bed at night and look to the sky and
plead with the powers above to shake you from
my core
To tear you from the fiber of my being that you
have rested so well within
An undetected foreign object who so closely
mimicked the fabric of my heart that my brain
just knew you were a vital piece
You have not ruined my thirst for love, but you
came close

End to Begin

Catch me in the midst of it all
Silent and firmly planted
Eyes fixated on things beyond sight, but
promised in words spoken long before my
existence
I am chosen
I am a creation that was designed with a purpose
in mind
I am the greatest example of love and the
simplest example of God's majesty
I forget this at times
I neglect my inner being and succumb to the
false realities of this world
But here in this moment I scream…
I AM
And with that, I can begin to be…simply me